T0052848

Compound Word

by Trisha Speed Shaskan
illustrated by Sara Gray

PICTURE WINDOW BOOKS
Minneapolis, Minnesota

compound word two words put together to make one word with a new meaning

Editor: Christianne Jones
Designer: Hilary Wacholz
Page Production: Melissa Kes
Art Director: Nathan Gassman
The illustrations in this book
were created with acrylics.

Picture Window Books
1710 Roe Crest Drive
North Mankato, MN 56003
www.capstonepub.com

Copyright © 2009 by Picture Window Books,
a Capstone imprint. All rights reserved.
No part of this book may be reproduced
without written permission from the publisher.
The publisher takes no responsibility for the
use of any of the materials or methods described
in this book, nor for the products thereof.

Library of Congress Cataloging-in-Publication Data
Shaskan, Trisha Speed, 1973-
If you were a compound word / by Trisha Speed
Shaskan ; illustrated by Sara Gray.
p. cm. — (Word fun)
Includes index.
ISBN 978-1-4048-4771-2 (library binding)
ISBN 978-1-4048-4776-7 (paperback)
1. English language—Compound words—Juvenile
literature. I. Gray, Sara, ill. II. Title.
PE1175.S43 2008
428.1—dc22 2008006352

Looking for compound words?

Watch for the BIG words throughout the book.

Special thanks to our advisers for their expertise:
Rosemary G. Palmer, Ph.D., Department of Literacy
College of Education, Boise State University

Terry Flaherty, Ph.D., Professor of English
Minnesota State University, Mankato

Printed in the United States 5735

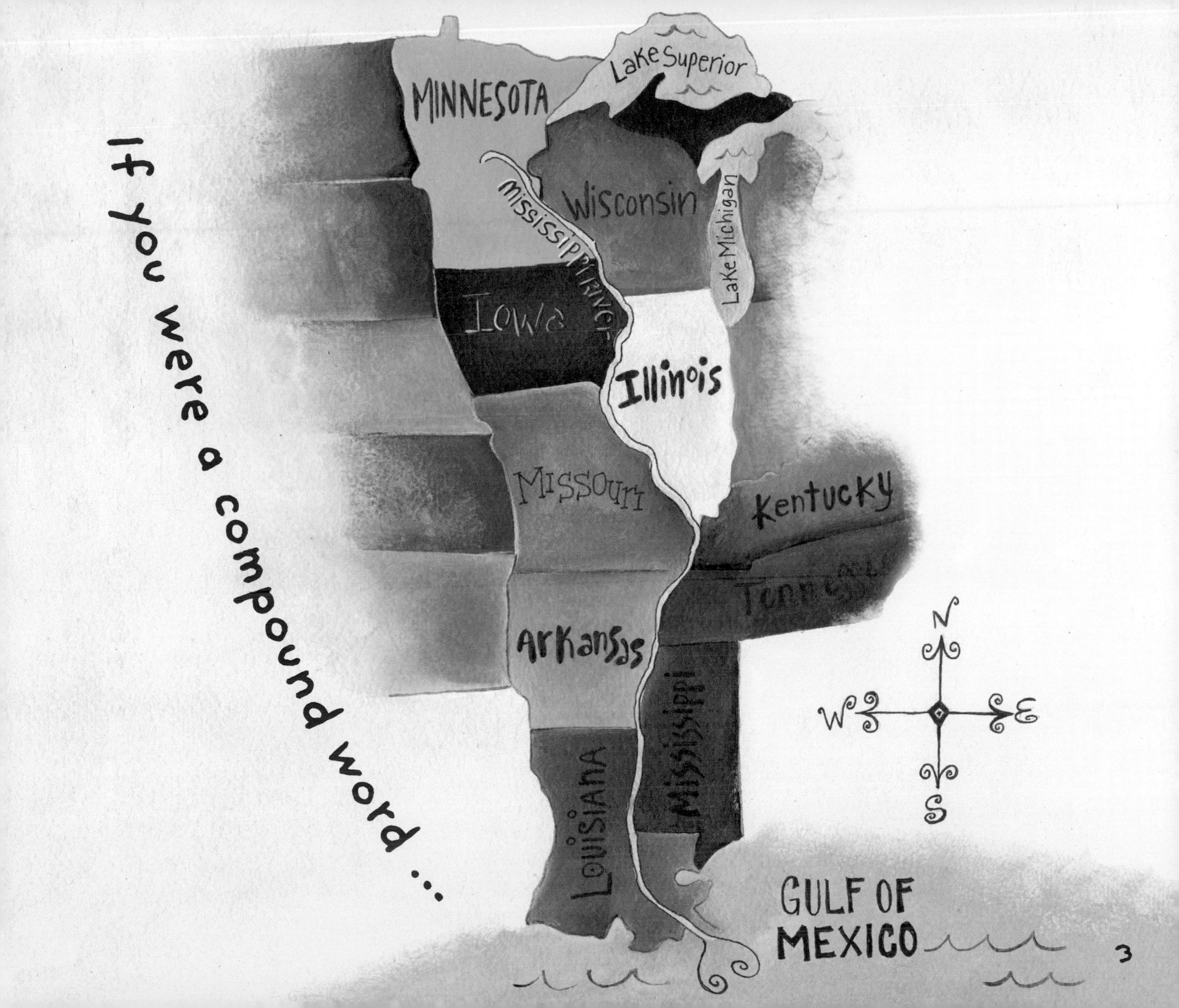
If you were a compound word ...
MINNESOTA
Lake Superior
Wisconsin
Mississippi River
Lake Michigan
Iowa
Illinois
Missouri
Kentucky
Tennessee
Arkansas
Mississippi
Louisiana
N
W
E
S
GULF OF MEXICO

... you could be a SWASHBUCKLER or a SHIPMATE traveling on a **SOUTHBOUND STEAMBOAT** down the Mississippi River.

If you were a compound word, you would be two words put together to make one word with a new meaning.

At the **HEADWATERS** of the Mississippi River in Minnesota, a **DRAGONFLY** rests on a **SANDBAR.**

If you were a compound word, you could have fun in any season.

During the **SUMMERTIME** in Minnesota,
a **BULLFROG** swishes through the **SEAWEED.**

During the **WINTERTIME** in Wisconsin, cows ice-skate across the frozen **WATERWAY** and play in SNOWDRIFTS.

If you were a compound word, you could be a form of transportation.

In Iowa, a bass family runs out of gas while relaxing on a **HOUSEBOAT.**

They don't call a
MOTORBOAT or a SAILBOAT.
They call a TOWBOAT.
TOWING

If you were a compound word, you could be a playful animal.

In Missouri,
WOODCHUCKS leave their
burrows to **SUNBATHE.**

Two JACKRABBITS play LEAPFROG in the grass.

If you were a compound word, you could describe the weather.

In Illinois,

THUNDERCLAPS boom!

A **RAINSTORM** floods the river
and rocks the boats.

If you were a compound word, you could be an animal enjoying different kinds of music.

In Kentucky, a **SOFTSHELL** turtle plays **BLUEGRASS.**

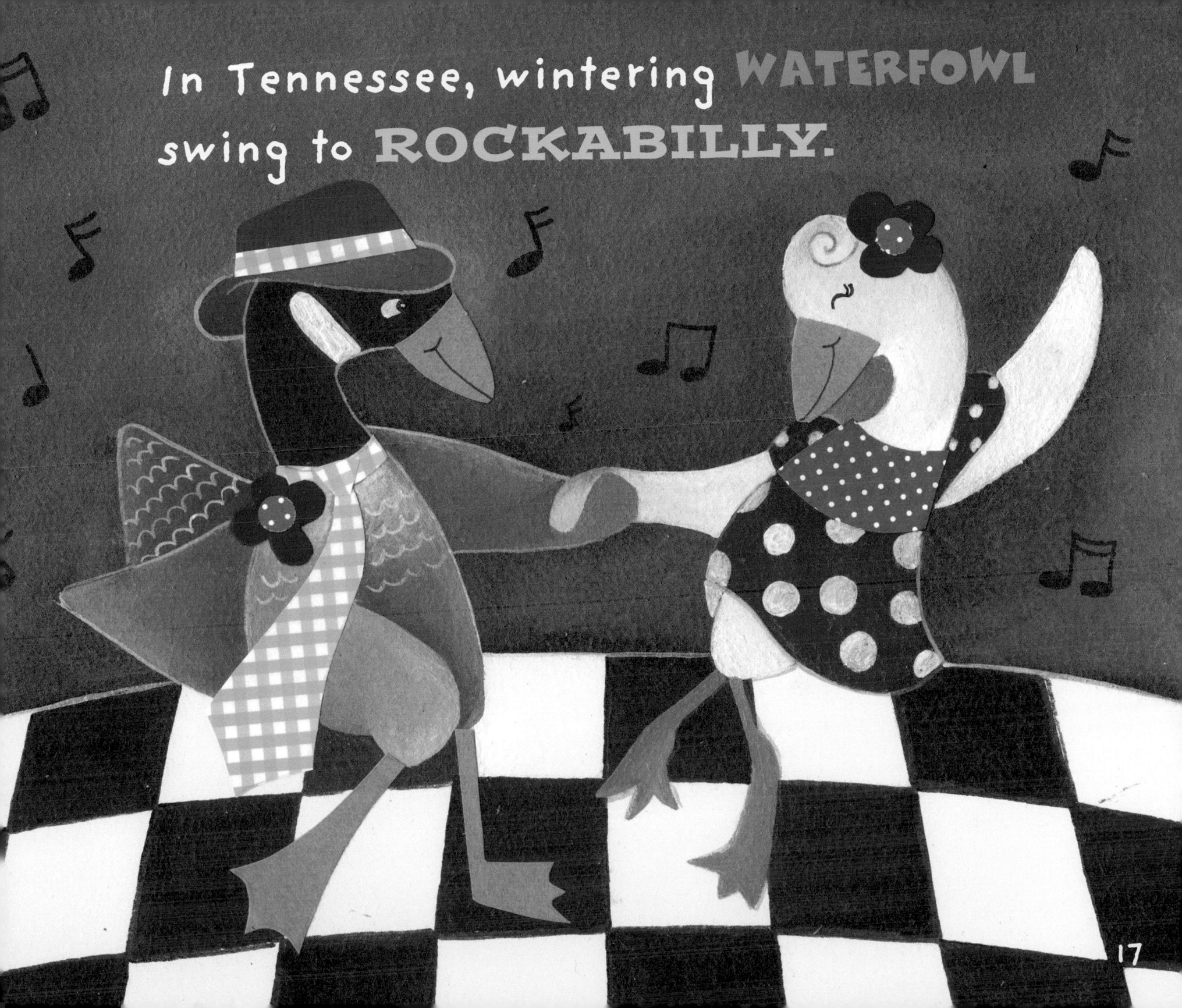

In Tennessee, wintering **WATERFOWL** swing to **ROCKABILLY.**

If you were a compound word,
you could describe nature.

In Arkansas, **SONGBIRDS**
play in the **HARDWOOD** forest.
Then they rest in the **GRASSLANDS.**

In Mississippi, trumpet **HONEYSUCKLES** sound their horns. **MAYPOPS** spin like **PINWHEELS.**

If you were a compound word, you could be different types of food.
In Louisiana, an alligator eats CRAWFISH pie and HUSHPUPPIES.

His daughter eats a CATFISH sandwich.

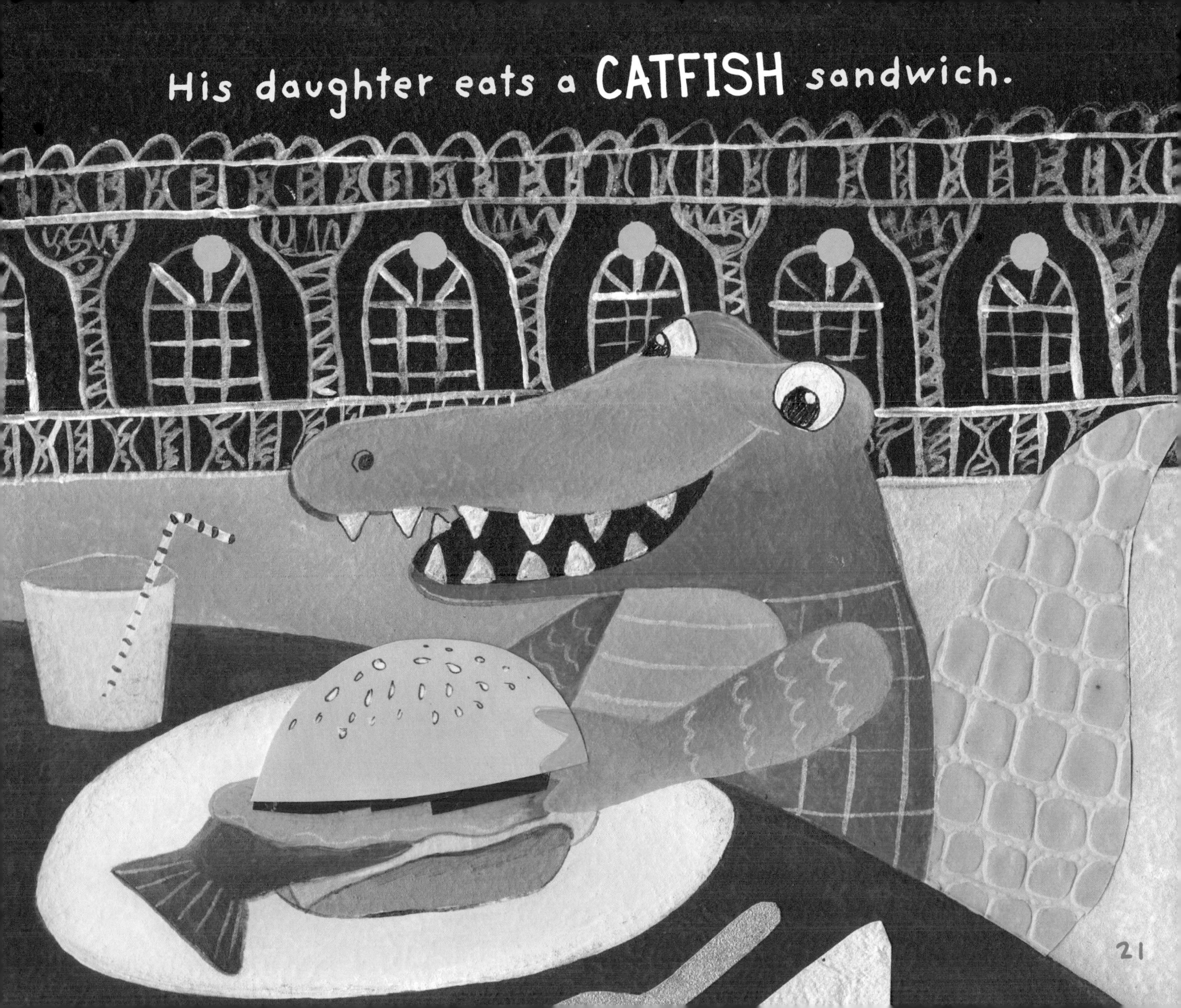

You could put things together and dream about a **LIFETIME** of **CAREFREE** adventures ...

... if you were a compound word.

MAKING YOUR OWN COMPOUND WORDS

Here are two lists of words that can become compound words when joined together. Join each word from the left column with a word from the right column. For example, *night* plus *gown* becomes *nightgown*. Use a dictionary to check if the word you made is a compound word. After you have created the compound words, write a story using all of them!

wind	storm
night	fall
bull	pour
rain	gown
down	frog

Glossary

compound word—two words put together to make one word with a new meaning
definition—the meaning of a word
headwaters—the beginning of a stream
swashbuckler—an adventurer

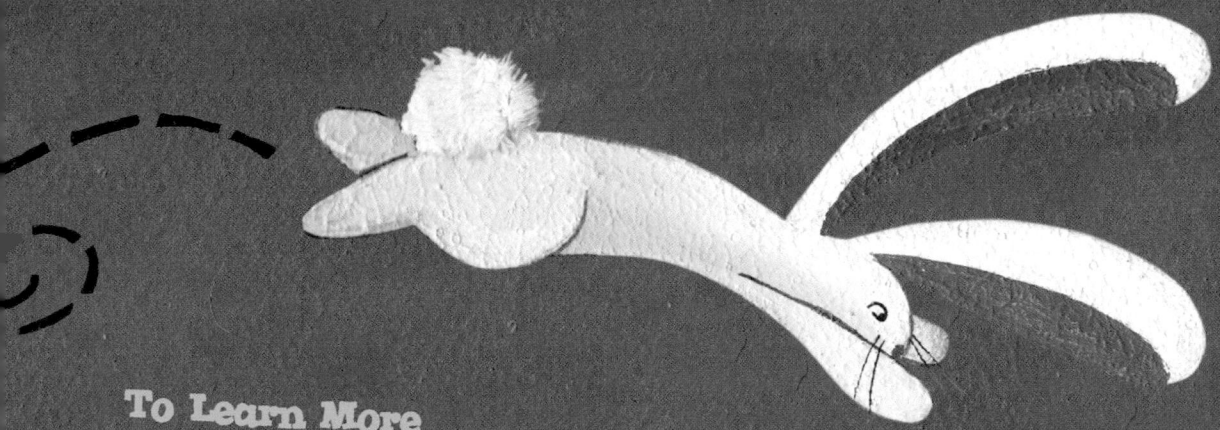

To Learn More

More Books to Read

Maestro, Betsy. *All Aboard Overnight.* New York: Clarion Books, 1992.

Rondeau, Amanda. *Base + Ball = Baseball.* Edina, Minn.: Abdo, 2004.

Walton, Rick. *Once There Was a Bull...frog.* Salt Lake City: Gibbs Smith Publishers, 1995.

On the Web

FactHound offers a safe, fun way to find Web sites related to topics in this book. All of the sites on FactHound have been researched by our staff.

1. Visit *www.facthound.com*
2. Type in this special code: 1404847715
3. Click on the FETCH IT button.

Your trusty FactHound will fetch the best sites for you!

Index

compound word
- as a season, 8-9
- as an animal, 12-13, 16-17
- as food, 20-21
- as music, 16-17
- as nature, 18-19
- as transportation, 10-11
- as weather, 14-15
- definition, 6

Look for all of the books in the Word Fun series:

If You Were a Compound Word
If You Were a Conjunction
If You Were a Contraction
If You Were a Homonym or a Homophone
If You Were a Noun
If You Were a Palindrome
If You Were a Prefix
If You Were a Preposition
If You Were a Pronoun
If You Were a Suffix
If You Were a Synonym
If You Were a Verb
If You Were Alliteration
If You Were an Adjective
If You Were an Adverb
If You Were an Antonym
If You Were an Interjection
If You Were Onomatopoeia